# Go Back to Sleep

## "VUELVE A DORMIR"

**Written by Jeannette Angel**

ISBN: 978-0-578-35161-2
Library of Congress Control Number: 2022930782

Design Artist: Don Trujillo
Interior design: Gary Trujillo
Bilingual in English & Spanish

Printed by DiggyPOD, Inc., in the United States of America.

First printing, 2022.

KLET & J LLC, Publisher
733 NE 204th St.
Seattle, WA 98155
smbizcs@hotmail.com

THIS BOOK IS DEDICATED TO
MY CHILDREN,
GRANDCHILDREN, GREAT GRANDCHILDREN
AND
MY PARENTS, JIM AND JOAN ANGEL

BIRDIES, BIRDIES
GO BACK TO SLEEP
I'M NOT READY TO MOVE MY FEET
YES, I HEAR YOU CHIRPING
IN THE TREES
BUT I STILL HAVE
DREAMS TO DREAM
AND
SNORES TO SNORE
BIRDIES, BIRDIES
GO BACK TO SLEEP

PAJARITOS, PAJARITOS
VUELVAN A DORMIR
NO ESTOY LISTO PARA MOVER
MIS PIES,
SÍ, TE ESCUCHO PIAR
EN LOS ÁRBOLES
PERO TODAVÍA TENGO SUEÑOS
PARA SOÑAR
Y
RONCAS PARA RONCAR
PAJARITOS, PAJARITOS
VUELVAN A DORMIR.

DOGGIES, DOGGIES
GO BACK TO SLEEP
I'M NOT READY TO MOVE MY FEET
YES, I HEAR YOU BARKING
IN THE YARDS
BUT I STILL HAVE
DREAMS TO DREAM
AND
SNORES TO SNORE
DOGGIES, DOGGIES
GO BACK TO SLEEP

PERRITOS, PERRITOS
VUELVAN A DORMIR
NO ESTOY LISTO PARA MOVER
MIS PIES
SÍ, TE ESCUCHO LADRAR
EN LOS PATIOS
PERO TODAVÍA TENGO SUEÑOS
PARA SOÑAR
Y
RONCAS PARA RONCAR
PERRITOS, PERRITOS
VUELVAN A DORMIR

CRICKETS, CRICKETS
GO BACK TO SLEEP
I'M NOT READY TO MOVE MY FEET
YES, I HEAR YOU CHIRPING
IN THE GRASS
BUT I STILL HAVE
DREAMS TO DREAM
AND
SNORES TO SNORE
CRICKETS, CRICKETS
GO BACK TO SLEEP

GRILLOS, GRILLOS
VUELVAN A DORMIR
NO ESTOY LISTO PARA MOVER
MIS PIES
SÍ, TE ESCUCHO CHIRRIAR
EN EL CÉSPED
PERO TODAVÍA TENGO SUEÑOS
PARA SOÑAR
Y
RONCAS PARA RONCAR
GRILLOS, GRILLOS
VUELVAN A DORMIR

PIGGIES, PIGGIES
GO BACK TO SLEEP
I'M NOT READY TO MOVE MY FEET
YES, I HEAR YOU OINK, OINKING
IN YOUR PENS
BUT I STILL HAVE
DREAMS TO DREAM
AND
SNORES TO SNORE
PIGGIES, PIGGIES
GO BACK TO SLEEP

CERDITOS, CERDITOS
VUELVAN A DORMIR
NO ESTOY LISTO PARA MOVER
MIS PIES,
SÍ, TE ESCUCHO GRUÑIR
EN TUS CORRALES
DE LOS CERDOS
PERO TODAVÍA TENGO SUEÑOS
PARA SOÑAR
Y

RONCAS PARA RONCAR
CERDITOS, CERDITOS
VUELVAN A DORMIR

FROGGIES, FROGGIES
GO BACK TO SLEEP
I'M NOT READY TO MOVE MY FEET
YES, I HEAR YOU CROAKING
IN THE POND
BUT I STILL HAVE
DREAMS TO DREAM
AND
SNORES TO SNORE
FROGGIES, FROGGIES
GO BACK TO SLEEP

RANITAS, RANITAS
VUELVAN A DORMIR
NO ESTOY LISTO PARA MOVER
MIS PIES
SÍ, TE ESCUCHO CROAR
EN EL ESTANQUE
PERO TODAVÍA TENGO SUEÑOS
PARA SOÑAR
Y
RONCAS PARA RONCAR
RANITAS, RANITAS
VUELVAN A DORMIR

OWLS, OWLS
GO BACK TO SLEEP
I'M NOT READY TO MOVE MY FEET
YES, I HEAR YOU HOOT HOOTING
IN THE TREE
BUT I STILL HAVE
DREAMS TO DREAM
AND
SNORES TO SNORE
OWLS, OWLS
GO BACK TO SLEEP

BÚHO, BÚHO
VUELVA A DORMIR
NO ESTOY LISTO PARA MOVER
MIS PIES,
SÍ, TE ESCUCHO ULULAR
EN LOS ÁRBOLES PERO
TODAVÍA TENGO SUEÑOS PARA SOÑAR
Y
RONCAS PARA RONCAR
BÚHO, BÚHO
VUELVA A DORMIR

KITTIES, KITTIES
GO BACK TO SLEEP
I'M NOT READY TO MOVE MY FEET
YES, I HEAR YOU MEOWING
IN YOUR BED
BUT I STILL HAVE
DREAMS TO DREAM
AND
SNORES TO SNORE
KITTIES, KITTIES
GO BACK TO SLEEP

GATITOS, GATITOS
VUELVAN A DORMIR
NO ESTOY LISTO PARA MOVER
MIS PIES,
SÍ, TE ESCUCHO MAULLAR
EN TU CAMA
PERO TODAVÍA TENGO SUEÑOS PARA
SOÑAR
Y
RONCAS PARA RONCAR
GATITOS, GATITOS
VUELVAN A DORMIR

COWS, COWS
GO BACK TO SLEEP
I'M NOT READY TO MOVE MY FEET
YES, I HEAR YOU MOOOOOING
IN THE PASTURE
BUT I STILL HAVE
DREAMS TO DREAM
AND
SNORES TO SNORE
COWS, COWS
GO BACK TO SLEEP

VACAS, VACAS
VUELVAN A DORMIR
NO ESTOY LISTO PARA MOVER
MIS PIES,
SÍ, TE ESCUCHO MUGIR
EN EL PASTO
PERO TODAVÍA TENGO
SUEÑOS PARA SOÑAR
Y
RONCAS PARA RONCAR
VACAS, VACAS
VUELVAN A DORMIR

CHICKIES, CHICKIES
GO BACK TO SLEEP
I'M NOT READY TO MOVE MY FEET
YES, I HEAR YOU
CLUCK CLUCKING
IN YOUR COOP
BUT I STILL HAVE
DREAMS TO DREAM
AND
SNORES TO SNORE
CHICKIES, CHICKIES
GO BACK TO SLEEP

POLLITOS, POLLITOS
VUELVAN A DORMIR
NO ESTOY LISTO PARA MOVER
MIS PIES,
SÍ, TE ESCUCHO CLOQUEAR
EN TU GALLINERO
PERO TODAVÍA TENGO
SUEÑOS PARA SOÑAR
Y
RONCAS PARA RONCAR
POLLITOS, POLLITOS
VUELVAN A DORMIR

PONY, PONY
GO BACK TO SLEEP
I'M NOT READY TO MOVE MY FEET
YES, I HEAR YOU NEIGHING
IN YOUR CORAL
BUT I STILL HAVE
DREAMS TO DREAM
AND
SNORES TO SNORE
PONY, PONY
GO BACK TO SLEEP

CABALLO, CABALLO
VUELVA A DORMIR
NO ESTOY LISTO PARA MOVER
MIS PIES,
SÍ, TE ESCUCHO RELINCHAR
EN TU CORRAL
PERO TODAVÍA TENGO SUEÑOS
PARA SOÑAR
Y
RONCAS PARA RONCAR
CABALLO, CABALLO
VUELVA A DORMIR

LITTLE LAMB, LITTLE LAMB
GO BACK TO SLEEP
I'M NOT READY TO MOVE MY FEET
YES, I HEAR YOU BAAAAAING
IN THE FIELD
BUT I STILL HAVE
DREAMS TO DREAM
AND
SNORES TO SNORE
LITTLE LAMB, LITTLE LAMB
GO BACK TO SLEEP

CORDERO PEQUEÑO,
CORDERO PEQUEÑO
VUELVA A DORMIR
NO ESTOY LISTO PARA MOVER
MIS PIES,
SÍ, TE ESCUCHO BALAR
EN EL CAMPO PERO
TODAVÍA TENGO SUEÑOS PARA SOÑAR
Y
RONCAS PARA RONCAR
CORDERO PEQUEÑO,CORDERO PEQUEÑO
VUELVA A DORMIR

BABY SISTER, BABY SISTER
GO BACK TO SLEEP
I'M NOT READY TO MOVE MY FEET
YES, I HEAR YOU GIGGLING
IN YOUR CRIB
BUT I STILL HAVE
DREAMS TO DREAM
AND
SNORES TO SNORE
BABY SISTER, BABY SISTER
GO BACK TO SLEEP

HERMANITA, HERMANITA
VUELVA A DORMIR
NO ESTOY LISTO PARA MOVER
LOS PIES
SÍ, TE ESCUCHO REÍR
TU CUNA PERO TODAVÍA
TENGO SUEÑOS PARA SOÑAR
Y
RONCAS PARA RONCAR
HERMANITA, HERMANITA
VUELVA A DORMIR

NOW I'M READY TO MOVE MY FEET!!
GOOD MORNING BABY SISTER
GOOD MORNING! MY FRIENDS,
IN THE TREES
IN THE PONDS
IN THE FIELDS
IN THE YARDS

AHORA, ESTOY LISTO PARA MOVER
MIS PIES!
BUENOS DÍAS HERMANITA
BUENOS DÍAS MIS AMIGOS
EN LOS ÁRBOLES,
EN LOS ESTANQUES,
EN LOS CAMPOS
Y
EN LOS PATIOS

I hope you enjoy reading this book to your children as much as I enjoy reading it to my grandchildren.

*Jeannette Angel*

A special Thank you to my Publisher and Editor, Gary M, Trujillo, my artistic designer, Don Trujillo, my inspiration Mr. Santana, my sweet pea Aria, my family, and friends who inspire me every day to write about life's little moments.

www.ingramcontent.com/pod-product-compliance
Lightning Source LLC
Chambersburg PA
CBHW040303100426
42811CB00011B/1349